CAMP BULLETINS
FROM 1110

⎯⎯⎯⎯⎯⎯⎯⎯⎯⎯⎯⎯

Jane Lichty Pearson

Copyright © 2018 **Taking Flight Press**
16 Molas Drive, Durango, CO 81301

Camp Bulletins From 1110

ISBN: 978-0-692-06083-4

Jane Lichty Pearson

Editor: Elizabeth A. Green
Layout: Lisa Snider
Cover Painting: Kathleen Shadell

Start writing, no matter what.
The water does not flow until the faucet is turned on.
— *Louis L'Amour*

With profound gratitude to all who said,
"Keep Going."

I'm sitting at my computer here in my beloved town of Durango, Colorado, with close to eighty stitches in my head. An adventure up at Sig Creek behind Purgatory Mountain Resort didn't end so well, and I can't tell you how very grateful I am to be able to see with both eyes.

I had time to heal, be still, and think about everything—*everything*—when my eyes finally returned to near normal. I woke up about five this morning knowing how to finish this little book.

Finally.

I am one of so many Baby Boomers raised during the '50s.

Big Bob and Annie Bun-Buns, (yes, those were my folks that raised me at 1110 Freeborn Street in Austin, Minnesota) had a somewhat tough job of raising me right. Sometimes raising me was "tougher than picking fly poop out of pepper." (Dad's words, not mine.)

"Jane Ann! If bullshit were music you'd be a brass symphony!" he would often say to me. "RF" (same person as "Big Bob") was tougher than nails at times. Raising a girl was a brand new experience for Bob Lichty. It was trial and error, but we got through it somehow.

Like many Boomers, I grew up hearing, "You are not leaving this table until you clean up your plate!" or "We're only doing this because we love you!" or "I don't want to spank you but I will."

How about, "If I ever hear you use that word around here again, I'm going to wash your mouth out with soap"? But the worst was, "Just wait until your father comes home."

It wasn't until my father's death in 1994 that I started writing stories, probably as a way of dealing with the loss of a parent. Never could I have imagined that years and years later a pair of mud flaps that pulled out in front of me on the way to PJ's Market would impact me so much.

Now those stories that were filed away have morphed into . . . this.

Peppered with lessons, humor, and yes, a bit of BS, it's my way of saying "Thank you." The older I get, the more I see how so lucky and blessed I was to have those lessons that grew me up.

So, dear reader, enjoy these stories that give but a snapshot of growing up in that small town. In writing them, I realized the truth of the biggest lessons of all: you never know how your actions right now can powerfully affect so many countless others down the road.

To love, health, and peace wherever you may be,

— **Jane Lichty Pearson**
Durango, Colorado

PROLOGUE
"S'ment S'mickers" and Serendipity

2014

Being short is not always good, or is it? Looking back on that particular day I have to wonder. Driving on a quiet county road in my beloved town of Durango, I saw vistas of the looming Rocky Mountains, blue sky, and green meadows. I loved driving alone on this road to PJ's Market. I would open the window, crank up the music and sing as if I were auditioning for *American Idol*. (No chance of that happening. Ask my family.)

I had just finished up my rendition of "Deep River Woman" when a behemoth vehicle pulled out in front of me. Large mud flaps replaced vistas.

Nice. There goes the view.

I eased off the gas pedal and tried to think of something pleasant instead of being enormously perturbed.

Remember when Geoff was little and he used to call a cement mixer a "sment smicker"? The thought made my lips curl up in a smile. Our son's word never made it to *Webster's Dictionary* but it did in our family lexicon.

I kept on staring at the mud flaps. I followed them until I could turn off at PJ's Market. It was then I finally saw what I was meant to see.

Written in big, black, boldface letters was the name:

MCNEILUS

My mind leaped back to my years of growing up in Austin, Minnesota. That name was connected to my Dad.

RF.

Big Bob.

The one that I would try and buck every chance I could. I thought to myself,

Don't go there, Jane. Move on.

He's gone.

I know.

I wonder what happened to McNeilus? I'll Google him when I get back home.

Turning into the market parking lot, I happened to glance at the clock. The time read "11:10."

There it was again.

The last time I was with my mom before she died was on November 10, 2011.

11-10-11.

1110.

The very number that still sits, percolates, and marinates in my gut. I see it when I glance at the clock at home, or the Garmin telling me how many steps I have taken so far. It brings back the voice that still echoes in my mind, the voice that would say, "Keep it up and we can go downstairs and lock horns!" or, "Because I said so, that's why."

It's a voice that my mind still fights with on occasion.

You are enough as is. Believe it.

Move and get the pork tenderloin in the crock-pot. You have to pick up the grandkids in an hour.

Driving back home I didn't notice the green meadows and blue sky. The memories of years ago blurred that vista. Groceries hastily put away, the pork tenderloin seasoned and parked in the slow cooker, I still had time to Google a name before picking up those kids that "Big Bob" never got to meet.

Hunches. The internal whisper I listened to changed so much for me that day.

A Fall Friday

1957

Camp Bulletins

"Open up window, let out sin. Let the little sunshine in!" he sings in his loudest voice. He yanks up the window shade, flooding my bedroom with light. There he stands in his plaid boxers. I can tell he's feeling the potential of a new day.

"Dad!" I yell, as I pull the blanket over my head. "My alarm didn't even go off yet!"

"Well, if you get up now you get the bathroom first."

I throw the covers off and glare at him. I'm not a morning person but my father does make sense. Sharing one bathroom with the family in the mornings is anything but fun. To be first ahead of the other siblings is a good thing.

I plod down the hall and am relieved to find that the bathroom door is open. The bath mat lying on the black and white little hexagonal tiles is still damp. I can see the imprints "Bear Tracks Lichty," my flat-footed father, makes after he steps out of the shower. The lingering smell of his Mennen after-shave lotion hangs in the air. The toilet seat is down, thanks to my mother's admonitions.

I shut the door and lock it and make my way to the small sink. I stand on my tiptoes to see freckles and a huge tangle of auburn hair reflected back to me. My blue eyes are far from sparkly at the moment. My thoughts go back to the night before when Dad came home from work.

I just wanted to talk to him. Why does he always say, "Not now, Jane!"?

Ok. So maybe he can't be like Ward Cleaver. Maybe he could try to be more like Dr. Anderson. I don't hear him barking orders at Ann Lee.

I ask my mother many times why Dad is the way he is.

Her answer is always the same.

"He is thinking about a very important decision he has to make at the bank, Janie."

"Why can't he just tell me that instead of just saying, 'Not now!'?"

She doesn't answer. I don't think Mom even knows what to answer.

I still don't get why he has to be so hard on us and why he can't just say "good job" once in a while?

"Jane Ann! Breakfast!" The command booms up the stairs as I put finishing touches on getting as beautified as I can for the day.

My ponytail isn't right! I don't like the skirt. Maybe the jumper Mom made would look better.

"Jane! Now! Your mother has breakfast on the table!" I cringe at the order, the Camp Bulletins that spew from his mouth like lava from Vesuvius. I feel for the people that work for him at the bank.

Breakfast at 1110 Freeborn Street is not an option.

Be there.

On time.

Better yet, ten minutes early.

He's commanding even at breakfast. Polished wingtips,

blue print tie lying flat against a white starched shirt—perfectly pressed by Mrs. Wallenberg—he's the vision of a man in charge. He peers over his glasses at me as I hustle to sit down, jumper on, ponytail off-center, and shoes in hand. The look in his eyes makes my gut clench.

Mom takes her place at the Round Dining Room Table. This is the only real wood table in the entire country that has Formica on it. Mom ordered it that way. No one else thought of putting Formica over beautiful cherry wood until Ann Lichty did. That table is not only one of a kind, it's virtually indestructible.

"Oatmeal and prunes again, Mom?" I ask.

Prunes. Mom's go-to remedy to ensure things run smoothly, so to speak.

Mom's breakfasts are infinitely better than some of the breakfasts she had to down. Living on the farm all she heard was "Waste not, want not." Even if it was a cornmeal and water concoction her mother made in the old family mush pan, they ate what was plated. Mush made Mom gag though, so it was tough to get down the hatch.

"The next morning my mother would make little patties from the leftover mush, fry them up in butter until they were brown and crispy," she told me. "Now those were good, especially with syrup poured over them!"

"Hey Blubber butt, pass the sugar!" says the One-That-Can-Rattle-My-Cage-More-Than-Anyone.

Brothers. I glare across the Round Dining Room Table

at my one and only one, named Alan.

"Who peed in your Post Toasties?" I retort.

"Kids! Enough!" Dad barks.

Oops. Here comes the "If you want, we can go downstairs and lock horns!" tone of voice.

Once again, the image of Ward Cleaver pops in my thoughts. Ward would never, ever think of locking horns with his children.

"Alan, it's your turn to choose a prayer from the prayer book," Mom says. Betsy-the-Younger is usually off the hook. She watches and listens to the dynamics of her two older siblings and usually makes a mental note not to go where we have trod.

This is a daily ritual at our house. Mom got this little book of prayers at our church in 1947, the year after I was born. We choose a prayer before breakfast each morning and then again before dinner.

We must need a lot of Divine Intervention at 1110.

Alan takes the blue prayer book and looks at a page.

I give him the "I-Hate-You-More-Than-Anything" look as he chooses the Morning Prayer to read.

"Wise and loving Heart," my brother reads, "to whom we give thanks for all good, give us wisdom and love in our hearts. We pray that we may be kind and thoughtful in all our dealings with others. We thank you for the ties of love that bind us together here. Help us always to be good to each other. In Jesus's name, Amen."

Got that Brother? We're supposed to be GOOD to each other.

Right.

Putting away the prayer book, Mom attempts to steer table conversation towards a more favorable family bonding experience.

Ann Lichty would have been a great stand-in for Ward Cleaver's wife, June, on the *Leave It to Beaver* show. June shows up once a week on our little black and white TV with perfect hair, heels, nylons, ironed dress, and apron.

Just like Mom!

The table is always magically set at the Cleaver household.

Yep. Just like ours.

Only nice, happy conversation is what I hear on TV during the show. Voices are never raised, and the Cleaver family is calmed and renewed by every dining experience.

Nope. Not even close.

"Anyone care for some brown sugar on their oatmeal?" Mom offers. She hates disharmony, and I can't pass up the brown sugar.

I heap on a good amount and mix it into the hot oatmeal. I barely have enough time to eat it all and stuff another prune in my mouth before the Camp Bulletins start.

Each day at breakfast, Dad issues these commands to "help" us organize our day, better our lives, hone our skills, and lead us down the Path of Perfection. They usually start after his morning coffee and breakfast, just before he needs to leave 1110 for his other home: The Bank.

Mom is not immune to them either. Her Camp Bulletins usually are questions.

"What's for dinner?"

That Camp Bulletin cracks me up. How can he be thinking about dinner when he just got full from breakfast?

"Did you call and make an appointment with Doc Leebens?"

"What time are Strongs coming over for dinner?"

"Did you record the deposit I put into your account?"

I hate Camp Bulletins. They make my insides constrict like a shirt going through the old wringer washing machine Myrtle Watson has in her basement across the street.

Betsy-the-Younger never gets Camp Bulletins. That also causes some angst for me. He slurps another sip of coffee and sets the cup in the saucer. His eyes narrow behind his glasses as he starts the next barrage. Alan is the target this time.

"Get your homework done after wrestling."

"How are you getting home after practice?"

"That grade in algebra needs to come up."

I wonder how he can he say so much in one breath.

Then it's my turn.

"Did you make your bed?"

"Practice the piano after school before you go outside."

"Get your room cleaned up. Don't shove your clothes

under the bed."

I wonder how my dad got to be Boss-of-Everyone. He was different when he was little, according to some stories we heard around the Dining Room Table when Uncle Max and Aunt Katherine came to visit. Max is Dad's younger brother. Mom and Dad had served cocktails before dinner. Uncle Max really enjoyed them. He started telling stories of growing up with my dad in Orange Township, Iowa, back in the '20s.

"Your dad," Max recounted, "would hypnotize chickens. He'd lay them out in the yard much to our mother's disgust. Then he'd go and hide in the plush, two-holed outhouse to get out of work around the farm."

Yuk.

The story of Dad giving Mom a hickey when she was sixteen was more than I could handle. I wonder how my mother could have been the least bit interested in some cocky kid with curly auburn hair named "Fay Lichty." I had to ask her.

"It was because of the four-leaf clover, honey."

"Mother took me with her to the cemetery by the church where we lived. Your grandmother told me when I was about thirteen to find a four-leaf clover and put it in my shoe. The legend was that the first man you saw would be the man you would marry."

"Guess what? The first man I saw was your father—but

at the time he wasn't high on my list."

"Why not?"

"He had fat fingers and flat feet. But he was really cute."

That cute, flat-footed, fat-fingered farm kid now sits at the Round Dining Room Table. He's all grown up and he's a banker. He gives orders at the bank, and he continues when he comes home. He is "Control King Extraordinaire" and totally unaware of the wake of constricted innards he leaves behind.

*How I wish I would have
known then what I know now,
that when someone rides your butt, it
COULD mean ... they care.*

A knock at the front door interrupts the litany.

"Connie!" says Mom in her June Cleaver voice. "Jane's just finishing breakfast so come in!"

I should know that my Freeborn Street chum would be early to pick me up on her way to school. She loves school. It's a reprieve from her tiny house crammed with a lot of kids one block away from 1110.

"You ready?"

I frantically push my feet into my saddle shoes, grab my jacket, say my goodbyes, and shut the front door as we head down the front walk.

"Good timing!" I say matter-of-factly as I try to keep up her pace. Two Jane steps equal one Connie step.

"Why?"

"Because. That's why."

I don't feel like going into the breakfast routine. Sometimes I think Connie is lucky not to have a bossy dad.

My ponytail swings as we walk next door to pick up Francie. We pass the expanse of lawn between our houses that surrounds the "forest," the grouping of pines and bushes that grow taller each year.

I look wistfully at the bare patch of ground that sits on the property line between her house and mine. Our lawns are green and lush—except for that spot.

When boys fight, they just duke it out and move on. Some girls do that too. Not Francie and me. When we have any kind of disagreement we march to the property line and pull grass on the other's lawn. No, I don't remember why pulling each other's grass was the ultimate insult when we were younger.

Stupid, I know.

Connie and her dimples are ahead of me, as usual.

She runs the fastest, kicks the farthest, and looks the cutest.

She also doesn't have a mother who blows TOOT TOOT...TOOT TOOT TOOT TOOT on the whistle when it's time to come inside.

And Francie? She's a blond beanpole with legs going up to her ears. The short, squatty body I get from my Pennsylvania Dutch lineage puts me at a disadvantage. I learn to walk fast to keep up with long-legged friends.

We knock on Francie's door.

"Mich!" Connie yells as she calls out her nickname. "Are you ready?"

"Give me a minute" She takes the stairs to the left of the front door to retrieve her jacket.

I see Mrs. Michie, Francie's mother, sitting at the red kitchen booth doing another crossword puzzle. Her mom uniform is a housecoat and slippers. Magnifying glasses perched on her nose, she is almost always doing crossword puzzles, or typing, or having coffee with my mother when all of us go to school and Dad leaves for work at the bank. What is said at those coffee hours is never shared with us.

Francie's mom walks out of the kitchen to greet us.

"I'm making Mockle Gropple for dinner tonight and there's plenty. Would you like to join us?"

Yes!

Mrs. Michie knows I love this one-dish dinner that she makes. The marriage of flavors: hamburger, onion, canned diced carrots (use only half of the juice), canned kidney beans, and canned tomato soup all served with canned applesauce beats Mom's open-faced Spam sandwiches, hands down.

Sorry Mom.

Canned anything reigns supreme on Freeborn Street. Both the Michie pantry and the Lichty pantry are stocked with a lot of cans, especially those cans that have "Campbell" on the label. Campbell's Tomato soup, Campbell's Cream of Mushroom (or Cream of Celery) soup, Campbell's Chicken Noodle soup, all are stacked neatly next to canned beans, canned vegetables and fruit, not to mention the canned Spam. I believe Mom's canning days growing up in Orange Township are long gone.

And Spam?

It's a staple on most Austin housewives' grocery lists. The advantages to having canned Spam are many. Not only does Spam have a shelf life of maybe 3,000 years, but you can eat it in thousands of different ways. Raw, fried, baked, diced, grated, Spam does it all. Fried Spam, deviled Spam, Spam Surprise, Spam Loaf, Sushi Spam, or even dressed up as Inez Butler's Spam En Casserole—the options are endless. Every soldier in military action can applaud, or curse, Mr. Hormel for creating this protein wonder. Every can of Spam made will forever have "Made in Austin, Minnesota" printed on it.

I wonder if the Hormel Plant wasn't in Austin, if Austin would still be like Austin.

Tonight, however, there is a lovely alternative to even the possibility of Spam for dinner at 1110. I am all over that possibility.

I love Mrs. Michie. She is like another mother to me. She talks *to* me and not down at me. It's a miracle in itself that she still talks to any of the Lichtys after . . . The Accident.

It happened not too long after we had moved to Freeborn Street. Mom told me the story years later of what had happened.

"Your dad and Martin Michie were going to Huntting Grain Elevator to check on some things. Your dad was driving and Mr. Michie was in the passenger seat. It was winter time and the roads were so slick.

She paused as her mind replayed a very painful scene. Tears welled up in her eyes as she tried to get the rest of the words out.

"There was a truck that couldn't stop at the stop sign. It T-boned the car . . . and it hit the passenger side where Mr. Michie sat."

Tears were rolling down my mother's cheeks. I knew what would come next.

"Mr. Michie was thrown out of the car, into a ditch. Dad crawled over to him, even with a broken leg. Mr. Michie died in your father's arms."

I handed her a hankie and hugged Mom tight.

"It was one of the hardest times your father and I faced, Janie. When I was in the hospital with him, he sobbed, it just broke my heart. They were gut-wrenching sobs."

I cried too, right then, not just for the loss of the father of my friend, but for my dad and mom too.

She continued. "He thought that it was his fault, and felt so guilty. That's when he told me we would probably have to move from this house. He didn't think Mrs. Michie and the kids would ever want to see him again."

"Move?"

I was shocked. To even think that we would have had to move again was a painful possibility. "What happened so that we could stay at 1110, Mom?"

"I think a miracle, and a wonderful heart in Mrs. Michie . . . she told me she wanted to have some time alone with Dad at the hospital.

"When I went back up to his room, he told me about that fateful visit with Marian."

She paused again as she thought back to that day.

"She told Dad that she had talked to the sheriff. She knew that there was nothing that Dad could have done to prevent getting hit. It wasn't his fault. The other driver was going too fast for conditions."

"She also told him that he'd best stay at 1110, because if there ever was a time that she needed him—for advice, for someone close by to help her with the kids—it was now."

So it was Marian Michie who got us to stay at 1110. No wonder I love her so much.

"Jane, belly up to the saw."
That's what Dad used to say when
something tough came my way.
Maybe he was thinking of
Mrs. Michie's visit after The Accident
when he gave me that advice.
I wish now I would have asked him.

Man Magnets and Cow Pies

We are now on perhaps the most beautiful block on Freeborn Street. Greta's block has a brick sidewalk going from one corner to the next all laid in a perfect herringbone pattern.

It must have taken someone forever to lay those bricks just so.

With giant oaks that stretch their limbs across Freeborn Street in front, Greta's white, gabled, bay-windowed house sits on a plush green carpet of lawn. This is the house of the Man-Magnet.

Yes. Man-Magnet.

The long legs, blondish hair, and Nordic features seem to attract every hormonally charged male to her. Even the way she walks is somewhat maddening to me. She reminds me of the long-black-robed nuns that walk up and down Kenwood Avenue to and from Pachelli Catholic School. They glide. Greta glides too.

Ok. Fine. I'm jealous.

Every time I am with her I am reminded of the time the cow pooped on my white organdy dress.

It had been an Easter dress like no other. It made me feel like Grace Kelly, Elizabeth Taylor, and Queen Elizabeth all rolled into one. The top was short-sleeved, navy linen. I loved how it contrasted with the full, white, organdy skirt. I felt like a princess when I put it on, and I could hardly wait to show it to the Tannreuthers after church in Orange Township. (They owned the farm across the road from Grandpa Clyde and Grandma Emma Bechtelheimer. Yes. That's really the name. And it took me many years to learn how to spell it. I was thankful for the last name of Lichty.)

As part of the "P and Relie" (Parents and Relatives) Easter gathering in this small rural community outside of Waterloo, Iowa, I would frequently visit the Tannreuthers to see what was going on with the cows and the pigs. I had wanted to get a farm-feeling fix that day, something I didn't have a chance to do in Austin.

The Tannreuthers were kind to me, so while the grownups talked at Grandma's I got permission to cross the road to the farm. It was a whole new world for me there. Cows to milk, eggs to gather from the hen house, all of it gave me the farm fix.

"Mr. Tannreuther! Where are you?" I had yelled as I went into his barn that Easter Sunday.

"Over here milking!" he replied. And sure enough, hunched over a pail was the Real Deal Farmer.

"Why, Janie! You here for Easter?"

"Yep," I replied, swishing the white organdy skirt just so, hoping he would notice my Easter dress.

"I thought I was in the way while everyone was cooking dinner. I wanted to come over and check out the calves."

If I had been wearing something else, I would have loved to put my fingers in the mouth of a calf and feel the strength of its suck. On that day, though, I just looked and talked with him about things that had happened since the last time I was at the farm.

As I turned to leave, I made the mistake of walking behind a cow. The one that was ready to poop. My white organdy skirt just happened to be in the way.

I never wore that Easter dress again.

That stain and my feelings of not being enough are one and the same in my mind, especially when it comes to Greta.

"Remember when Greta told on you in first grade, Jane, about eating the Elmer's white paste?" Connie reminds me as we cross the street.

Do you have to keep bringing that up, Connie?

And yes, I do remember. Greta saw me eating the paste and told Mrs. Campbell, our teacher. Mrs. Campbell took my hand and led me to the little room off of our classroom at Sumner School. There, she gently scolded and told me, "Janie, when you eat this glue it might make your insides stick together." I remained embarrassed the rest of the day.

I was furious at Greta for tattling.

The Not-Good-Enough-Demons work on my mind when we walk past the tree, the one that both Greta and Connie can climb like monkeys.

I do not have that gift. Every time I look up in the branches I remember Greta taunting me to, "Come on up, Buck-Teeth Buckaroo."

That was another lesson I should have learned back then, that you can discover more about a person in an hour of play than in a year of conversation. An hour of playing with Greta showed me I couldn't be as athletic, long-legged, or attractive as she was.
But an hour of playing with Greta should have taught me that the only tree climber standard I needed to measure up to was . . . my own.

Shredded Curtains

We head up the driveway to pick up Man-Magnet.

"Uftah," says Francie as I almost trip over a brick that sticks up by Greta's driveway. I smile when Francie says, "Uftah."

We go around to the back door and knock.

"Greta's mom must have made bread again," says Francie as she wrinkles up her nose. The smell of freshly made bread is definitely in the air. Most everything is made from scratch at the Strand household. I don't see cookies in the cookie jar or cans of anything in the kitchen.

"Come in girls!" Mrs. Strand answers in her very matter-of-fact voice. Everything about Greta's mom is that way. She is right to the point and not one you want to hug.

Greta is still sitting in the booth at the far end of the galley kitchen munching on the *gjetost* cheese on a thick slice of homemade bread. That Norwegian cheese is a traditional breakfast in most Norwegians' homes. Some slice the cheese thin. Not Greta. She slices that sweet cheese thick to put it on the bread.

I could eat a lot of that cheese but Mrs. Strand doesn't offer me any. I think she feels that I will like myself better if I'm not tempted by the offering.

Wrong.

Greta finishes the last bite and pats Mandy the dachshund goodbye for the day. We don't have a lot of time left to walk the remaining couple of blocks to Sumner School.

"We're going to be late!" says Connie.

Being late means a real phone call from the part-time principal Miss Cummings. (She is also the kindergarten teacher.) Miss Cummings is warm but firm. I learn to be very nice and polite around Miss Cummings. If she ever calls Mom and Dad about me misbehaving, being tardy or being ill-mannered, it won't be pleasant at home. Count on it.

"I can hardly wait to see *You're a Young Lady Now*. I'll just die if we have to see that with the boys in the auditorium," I say.

"Not to worry, Jane Ann. The boys have to stay in the classroom. We get to see the movie in the auditorium," says Greta.

"Who says?" I ask.

"Miss Erickson. Didn't you hear her?"

No, I didn't hear my teacher. I was preoccupied when she made the announcement. I was looking at the other teacher next door, Mr. Finley, watching Miss Erickson do the hula wearing the grass skirt she got from her trip to Hawaii. She was "rotating the crops" much to Mr. Finley's delight.

Miss Erickson, Mr. Finley, and Mrs. Josephine Blabaum (I love her name) wait outside their classrooms to greet all of us. Francie and I go to Miss Erickson's class, while Connie goes into Mrs. Blabaum's classroom. Greta goes into Mr. Finley's room and the male eyeballs again are glued to her.

"Say hello to Mrs. BLAAbahm" I say to Connie after putting my jacket in the hall locker.

We are safely in our seats when the bell rings. We aren't

tardy. My mind is on the film and I feel nervous. I wish I could be the one to take the attendance slip to the office but Miss Erickson chooses Lillian Gnocchi instead. We stand and say the pledge, and then sit down as Miss Erickson chooses someone other than me to pass out the *Weekly Reader*.

"Kids, when you get your *Weekly Reader*, please read the front page and be ready to answer the questions I have written on the blackboard."

I love the *Weekly Reader*. It's like a short edition of stuff I would read in the *Austin Daily Herald*.

I stare at the blackboard. Squinting, I make out the words in Miss Erickson's perfect cursive handwriting:

1. How long did it take Magellan to sail around the world and what year was it?
2. How long did it take the very first airship to go around the world? Who made it and how long did it take?
3. How long did it take the first non-stop American Air Force Boeing B-50 to go around the world and what year did it happen?

4. What was the country that first put a satellite in space that went around the world? How long did it take?

All of us have to write the questions on our papers, underline them, and then answer them in complete sentences.

Maybe we have to do this just to use up time before the movie.

That's OK by me. But I do learn that Russia sent the first space satellite to go around the world in just a fraction of the time it took Magellan to sail his ship around the world. The Space Race is on.

"Jane, make sure you put your name and date on the paper," Miss Erickson reminds me, as she picks up our papers and stacks them on her desk.

Wish we could go home right now. Or even have an "In Case of Attack Get Beneath Your Desk Drill." Even lining up for a polio shot would be better than seeing this movie!

None of the above happens.

"Ladies, please line up, go to the auditorium and take a seat. Gentlemen, you may line up to go to Mr. Finley's room."

I line up, thankful that the boys won't be joining us.

Filing into the Carnegie Auditorium, I try and sit by Francie and Connie but Sandy Stephenson glides into the remaining seat by them. I find a seat in front of them and sit down. I look straight ahead. Connie clears her throat and I look around at her. Maybe they are as embarrassed as I am.

Our school nurse, Mrs. Bulger, quietly stands up in the front of the auditorium where she has been sitting. She has those pamphlets in her hand and waits for us to get settled.

She asks us to be quiet before she starts. I slump more in the chair.

She starts talking about the changes that make our bodies go from plain to fancy. Giggles and blank stares greet Mrs. Bulger. I already know about this stuff. Mom had filled me in when Betsy-the-Younger came along.

The nurse quietly goes to the back of the auditorium and asks Sandy Stephenson to turn out the lights.

The auditorium darkens. The projector starts whirring *You're A Young Lady Now.* No one speaks, not once during the whole thing. It is quiet even when Sandy Stephenson flicks the lights back on after the film is over.

"Does anyone have any questions?" asks our school nurse.

Does she think that anyone is going to ask a question pertaining to *You're a Young Lady Now?* In front of everyone? I don't think so.

I'm done being embarrassed for the day. I am thankful when it's time to go to lunch and then out for recess. The girls in the "in-crowd" huddle in the playground corner gossiping and laughing, throwing glances at those "not in the in-crowd."

Guess what crowd I'm in?

I hate recess.

PE is the last class of the day. Teams are chosen for a game of kickball. I am the last to be chosen.

I hate PE.

"Finally," I exhale when the bell rings announcing the end of school.

I don't wait for any of the Freeborn Street Chums. The day is exhausting enough and walking four blocks home alone is fine by me. I count the cracks in the sidewalk on each block to keep from thinking about the day. Maybe I count the cracks in the sidewalk so I don't have to feel anymore.

Mom sees my ponytail swinging from side to side as I walk up the front steps to 1110.

Not a good sign for her. She knows that how the ponytail swings, there goes the day.

I slam the front door shut and throw some of the school papers on Dad's green chair. No one ever is supposed to put anything in Dad's green chair. It's like his throne or something.

"Not a good day today?" Mom asks in her best "I-wish-I-could-make-it-better" tone of voice.

Good thing she made another batch of gingersnaps. I need about a dozen to dunk in a glass of milk. I hope Bill-the-Milkman delivered during the day. I need a bunch of dunking liquid.

He did, and I dunk. I unload to Mom in the kitchen, sitting at the breadboards that pull out of the counter. Every insecure, unfair happening comes pouring out of my mouth as I drown my sorrows with each dunk.

Mom listens. She pulls out the breadboard next to me and sits down on the stool, the timer in her hand.

"OK. You've got ten minutes for a pity party. Lay it on thick. Then go up and change and practice your piano. You've got a lesson tomorrow!"

Her ability to maneuver not just me, but Dad as well is amazing. I don't know what kind of handbook she has read on "How to Parent," or for that matter "How to Live with Bob Lichty," but she knows exactly when to be quiet, when to slam cupboards or just say a few words that can pack quite a punch.

My bedroom curtains are a good case in point. Those pretty white ones that Mom sewed on the old Singer sewing machine for me.

Wonder when she is going to fix these? I ponder weeks after I had the big tantrum.

It had happened when I wanted to go outside and play Kick the Can in the alley with the neighborhood kids. Mom had stood firm and insisted on piano lessons and chores first.

I sassed her, which is not a good thing to do with Ann Lichty, much less with Bob Lichty. Mom stood firm. There was no budging her at that point.

"Go up to your room now, Jane, and do not come back down until you're ready to get the chores done!"

I had stormed upstairs to my room, slammed the door shut and lain on my bed.

The first thing I saw was the curtains—the pretty, white, eyelet lace ones that Mom had stayed up late one night to sew for my two bedroom windows. I got up off the bed.

I took my scissors and cut those curtains from the bottom to the top.

Yes. I did.

Over and over until each panel was in ten limp, crooked ribbons.

Mom never said a word. She let me live with those curtains, just as they were.

I had to look at them every single day thereafter. Hanging there in ten limp, crooked ribbons from the curtain rod that she had bought special for me.

Still, Mom never said a word.

I tried to fix them myself, carefully taking little gold safety pins that I had to buy in order to pin those ten limp curtain ribbons together as carefully as I could.

Mom would bring fresh clothes from the laundry room up to my room, and still, she never said a word.

*Neither Dr. Spock, nor any
child psychologist since, could have
imprinted such a valuable lesson on me
better than Annie, my mother.
All without saying a word.*

Do It on Your Own Manure Pile

My Pity Party is now over.

I change my clothes and my fanny finds its way to the piano seat. Opening up the music book containing Bach's Two- and Three-Part Inventions for the Piano, I curve my fingers and place them on the ivory keys. I play until I can get through the piece I was to practice without a mistake.

There is no "That sounded really nice," or "Good job!"

Nope.

Dad just comes in, takes the papers I had left on his chair and points to them.

I comply and put them away. Neat and tidy is the rule of the house, each and every day.

I watch him pour himself a stiff JB scotch and pick up the latest issue of *Time* magazine. That's what he does most nights after work. He pours a lot of scotch in his glass. He never measures how much scotch to put in, he just pours. Scotch is to him what gingersnaps are to me.

"Where's Mother?"

"I'm right here, Bob. I wasn't expecting you so early. I thought you were playing golf with Bob Gray today."

"I was. Ground at the golf course was harder than Kelsey's nuts, so Gray and I decided to try again on Saturday."

I make a note in my head to ask my dad sometime what Kelsey's nuts and hard ground have in common.

Then he gives me a look that clearly says, "I need to talk

to your mother alone."

I don't hear them talk. Dad sounds serious about something.

I go upstairs to my room with the latest issue of *Ladies Home Journal* in my hand. There are short stories in there and I like to read them. I am almost to the end of a great story when I hear another Camp Bulletin.

"Jane! Get down to help your mother set the table!"

So much for Mockle Gropple at Michies'.

I saunter downstairs and go into the kitchen to grab the place mats, silverware, and plates, fearful that Inez Butler's Spam En Casserole is for dinner. I put them on top of the Round Dining Room Table. "Where's Alan?" I ask as I put down the last fork.

"I told him to get washed up after wrestling practice, honey. He was a little on the smelly side."

What else is new?

I don't say it. I just think it.

Table set, Alan smelling like Dial soap and Old Spice aftershave, we all assume our designated spots and get ready to eat.

The Blue Prayer Book is sitting by Mom. She reaches for it and prays:

"O God, may our little family today be a true part of thy great family. May we be all one in spirit. Thou hast made us all different in body and all alike in soul. May we use all our differences to build stronger the unity of spirit

that makes us all one with each other and with thee. We thank thee, God, that we are all **so different and yet so alike.** Help us to be good to each other in our little family and to all others in thy one great family. Help us always to see through outer difference to inner alikeness. AMEN."

I know why she picked that one. Mom does that. She'll try and get a point across with the prayer she picks.

"What's for dinner?" asks Dad.

"Bob, you asked that at breakfast. It's Mim's Mess." says Mom.

It's a family favorite. Thanks to Mim Tenneyck, Mom and the girls at the Christian Sisters Bridge Club had been delighted to learn a new twist on hot-dishes that stretched the meat and got in the veggies. "It's easy," Mom had said the first time she made it. "You just layer raw hamburger, sliced onion, a bunch of Velveeta cheese, sliced green peppers, and some raw bacon and smother it with a can of tomato soup. Cover it, pop it in the oven, and put your feet up for a couple of hours."

Mom adds to the "mess" with sliced potatoes and about three tablespoons of rice.

Word has spread.

"Mim's Mess" even made it into the First Congregational Church cookbook. It's a hit especially at the Lichty household, served with applesauce on the side.

"Pass your plates to Dad, and he'll serve you up."

We all dig in, and see that Dad is in a very good mood.

"I ran into Catherine Boettcher today," says Mom, making conversation.

We were neighbors with them when we lived in the corner house on old Winona Street. They rented a house too. Then Boettchers got to move into their own house a couple of blocks away from 1110.

"How are Catherine and Ray?" says Dad.

"They're good. Catherine and I were talking about when we got to move into this house."

I knit my eyebrows together, and wonder what Boettchers have to do with us moving into 1110.

"No," she says, reading my face. "We were talking about how we got your Dad to change his mind about buying a house."

I perk up and listen as I have a second helping of Mim's Mess.

What I really want to know is how do you manage to budge Bob Lichty on any issue.

That's one thing about Mom. She can be persistent.

"How did you get Dad to change his mind, Mom?"

"Well, Dad told me one day after work that Bob and Alma Gray might sell their house on Freeborn Street. I just told him that I would be the happiest woman on earth if I could have that house.

"Bless Dad, he talked to them and arranged for us to go and see the house."

I sort of remember that day when Mom and Dad piled

Alan and me into the Studebaker to drive past this white two-story house.

I liked the big yard to play in and the pretty maple trees that bordered the street. I think I loved the screened in porch on the side of the house the most. It had a closet that you could crawl through to get into the garage.

More questions from me on how she got Dad to reconsider buying a house.

"I don't think it was the knotty pine kitchen or the wood-paneled family room. Maybe it was because Alma Gray had put a fire in the fireplace. It felt like home."

"I really liked the half-moon carved in the bathroom door downstairs." Dad says.

"I know why; because it was a flashback to the outhouses you liked to tip over, Robert," says Mom, smiling at him.

I love the story of the outhouses. Dad used to go and tip them over as a kid with his brother Max and then sneak behind the barn to puff on a celebratory corncob.

Dad's head must have been full of ideas on how to afford that house. Maybe some scotch helped lube all the dreaming and scheming he and Mom had to do.

That's the thing about Dad.

He is persistent, too. When he gets something into his head that won't go away, somehow, someway, he always seems to make it happen.

"You have to zero in on your target," he has told me

more than once.

"How long after that did you get the house?" I ask.

Dad leans back in his dining room chair.

"Oh, must have been about a week before I called Gray back and told him we should talk before any alternatives developed."

"How come you waited a week?" Alan asks.

"Because I was doing my homework. I paid FHA twelve bucks to get an appraisal price on 1110." Then he starts laughing.

"Damn thing is Bob Gray did the exact same thing. So when I called Gray up to arrange a meeting at the bank, we both had an idea of how much."

"Bob! Your language!" Mom looks at Dad with a look that says he better clean it up.

Dad taught me much later that whenever you make a deal, do it on your own manure pile. There are certain home advantages. That, and over-prepare, then go with the flow.

He cracked a slight smile as he remembered the day that Gray came into the bank after hours, shook hands, and made some small talk.

"What happened?" I asked.

"I offered him a cigar, and came to the point. I asked him what he was thinking of asking for the house. Gray gave me a number and I said, 'Too high.' So I countered."

Mom starts to laugh. "That's because everyone in Austin

Persistence wins.
That's the lesson I think of every time
I think of how we got 1110.

knows that if you can get a discount on a wholesale price you're a happy man!"

"True. So I gave him a lower number."

Betsy-the -Younger looks puzzled. "What's 'discount' mean?"

"It just means your father is frugal, dear, not spending any more than he has to for something."

However you look at it, my dad knows how to get a lot of mileage out of a buck.

Dad continues. "I told him we could just split the difference and call it good. Ten minutes later we had a deal."

Mom smiles. "That was one of the best days when Dad called to tell me the news. We got 1110 below appraisal and the Grays got the money they needed for the house Alma wanted to build."

She nods at me to get up and start clearing the dinner dishes away. Mom is still smiling at how everyone, the Grays and the Lichtys, all got what they needed.

Soaked Knickers

"What's for dessert?" asks Alan, looking towards the kitchen. As he turns to catch an early preview of what Mom might be bringing from the kitchen, he dumps his milk glass all over the front of his shirt.

Serves him right.

I stifle an urge to laugh uncontrollably. I can't help myself. The corners of my mouth just have to turn upwards.

"What's so funny? I just got soaked," he snarls at me.

"Both of you stop!" We both look to see our dad give us the "locking horns" look. He can't keep that look for long because cocktails before dinner always loosen him up.

Stories from growing up in Iowa are readily told. Dad's quite the story-teller, thanks to his Aunt Elsie from long ago. She made him take elocution lessons from her to help him get over his stuttering. She taught him well.

"Did I ever tell you kids the story of when I got baptized?"

Of course he has. About three hundred times but he has to tell the story again, about how at age thirteen, he decided it was time to be entered in the folds of the righteous and be baptized into eternal life. Everyone at the Church of the Brethren had to decide when the time was right for them to get dunked.

Yes. Dunked.

I just got my forehead sopped by Rev. Beale when I got baptized, according to Mom.

"Fats Lichty," as he was known, ran around with Perry "Skinny" Miller. What one couldn't think of, the other did.

"I decided first that I was ready to get dunked and then Skinny thought he would do it at the same time.

"I climbed into the buggy and off we went to church. Skinny was there waiting for me, and we walked up the front stairs of the church, met by Rev. Lichty."

My ears perk up.

"Rev. Lichty?" I ask.

Dad looks at me like I should know that everyone in Orange Township is related somehow.

Much to my chagrin my mother and my father are even distantly related.

Mom promises that I won't be a blithering idiot as they are maybe third or fourth cousins.

"I think it was Rev. Blough who dunked you, Bob," injects Mom sweetly as she brings out our parfaits. She is so proud of this dessert: arranged in a tall glass are a layer of crushed Vanilla Wafers, then a layer of vanilla pudding, a layer of sliced strawberries, and repeated if there is room.

I have to say it is a stunning presentation.

Dad stops the story while he digs his spoon into the parfait for one tasty bite and then another.

He starts to laugh. I see his belly go up and down. This is the best part of Dad's stories. He laughs until tears roll down his cheeks as he remembers a scene. The stories might not even be funny, but you know how it is when someone just starts laughing? I don't know about you, but I start laughing too.

"Mom told me to wear these God-awful old tweed

knickers on the day we got baptized. Skinny and I sat together—me in my itchy old knickers—and started laughing. Mother was ready to belt us, but we stopped when our names were called to walk down the aisle to the Baptistery."

"What's that?" asks Betsy-the-Younger.

"It's a big tank of cold water, sort of like a horse trough. We'd have to get dunked in it if we wanted our souls saved.

"So I got dunked in the name of the Father, the Son, and the Holy Ghost, and when I was done, I tried to leave the tank."

The tears start rolling down his cheeks as the memory plays out.

"Every time I tried to crawl out of the Baptistery, my pants would fall down. Trouble was that my knickers took on a lot of water, and they were heavier than a wagon full of shucked corn. Skinny had a hard time keeping a straight face when he saw the knickers almost at my ankles."

Now all of us are laughing. Dad tries to continue as he wipes away the tears, but he can't stop laughing. We can't either.

"Dad stepped in to pull my pants up at the last minute; otherwise I would have been mooning everyone who was at the service that morning!"

Stories continue even after everyone has finished the parfaits. Stories of running naked to jump in the horse trough and cool off on hot, humid Iowa summer days, or 4th of July gatherings in Tannreuthers' grove with homemade ice cream and a band, all were the stories of simpler days.

Thank the Lord for those rib ticklers and belly laughs. Without them, Camp Bulletins would have stung a whole lot more. That's the thing about humor and laughter; it softens and makes palatable the harshness that life can bring.

SATURDAY

1957

Rounds of Deliciousness

Saturdays.

Sleeping in, no one appearing early in the morning singing, "Open up window let out sin," pancakes—all make Saturday my favorite day of the week.

I stretch luxuriously under the covers, and then slowly pull them off. Gogi Grant's voice floats down the hall.

"The wayward wind is a restless wind..." I know these words by heart.

Wonder if he's going to play "Blueberry Hill" next?

Fats Domino, Pat Boone, and Danny and the Juniors are all making money thanks to Alan's growing collection of 45s. I like hearing the songs. I mouth the words to "Blueberry Hill" and dance down the hallway to the bathroom. *"I found my thrill on Blueberry Hill, on Blueberry Hill when I found you."*

The dancing got me to where I needed to go. Almost done with my business, I hear Mom's voice from the bottom of the stairs.

"Kids! Pancakes almost on the plates. Come and get them!"

Mom doesn't have to repeat the command. I finish, get out of my pj's, and change into play clothes. The aroma of pancakes, warmed maple syrup, and melted butter hasten my journey down the steps.

This is Mom's Saturday morning routine. Even before 1110 when we were in the rental on west Winona Street, she would invite any and every kid to come and have pancakes with us. For as long as I remember, there has always been room for "one more."

Dad's like this, too. It must be in the genes. Even his grandfather, who built a big, blue house long ago in Orange Township, had people and travelers stop and stay for a meal or a room. (I mean hospitality is in the genes, not building. Dad couldn't slice butter with a hot knife if he tried.)

I am the first at the table. I eagerly spear four of those light, delectable, round circles of absolute deliciousness from the platter and deposit them on my plate.

"Where's Dad?" I ask cautiously.

"He's at the Oak Leaf... for breakfast," Mom answers curtly.

Now the reason for the slammed doors is beginning to make sense. Slammed doors in the kitchen are a sign that Mom is not happy. She doesn't yell or scream because ladies aren't supposed to raise their voices. That rule on what's supposed to be "lady-like" doesn't apply to slamming doors, apparently.

I remember last night when I lay in bed, I thought I overheard them in their bedroom talking. Mom's voice sounded unhappy.

I think there is a good reason she says sometimes, "Do you love me or do you not? You told me once but I forgot."

"Blubber butt! Save some for me!" says Alan, interrupting my thoughts.

"Hey, you snooze you lose!" I say, wanting to take even more off the pancake platter.

"Kids, stop!"

There's that tone of voice that Mom has sometimes that just tells me it would not be a good idea to push her over the edge with anything. I do have to ask the question, however.

"How come he went out for breakfast?"

Mom gives me that look, wondering how much to share with us. She puts down her fork, and says, "Because he needs some quiet time. There are a lot of things going on at the bank."

That's one thing I can say about Bob the Banker. He's pre-occupied most of the time.

"Maybe he needs to go out for a game of golf," says Alan.

"That's what I think he intends to do after breakfast," Mom answers.

We all hope that if he does, he has a good day at the golf course. It's a given fact that how the golf score goes, there goes the day.

High score days are grueling for Dad. When he took up the game about five years ago he couldn't hit the broadside of a barn. He and the driving range bonded a lot. Mom says he doesn't hit the ball at right angles anymore.

"He hasn't hit any trees lately," says Mom.

All those trees at the golf course are Dad's fault. I didn't know it at the time but Dad had been approached at the bank about getting more trees to plant to make the course have more shade, and create more difficulty for fledgling golfers.

"He's sure missing out on these," I say as I pour the warmed syrup over another pile of pancakes.

I continue to consume deliciousness here at 1110.

"Keep on piling up those things on your plate, Thunder-thighs, and then you'll have to go downstairs and use the fat-melting jiggle machine."

Oh yes.

The Stauffer Home Magic Couch.

Mom was sold when she saw the article in *Ladies Home Journal* at Ramseth's Beauty Salon. She ordered one after talking Dad into making this investment for our health. All you have to do is lie down on this couch, buckle up, and flip the lever to "On."

"Magically, inches from your waist, hips, and thighs get jiggled away," she said as she tried to sell the concept to Dad.

Dad has a hard time parting with a buck. But when Mom persists, Dad can't resist. Mom persisted. We got the fat melting jiggle machine. (OK. So it hasn't worked its magic yet on my butt. It's still fun to lie, jiggle, and pretend that the magic will kick in soon.)

I ponder yet another pancake when the phone rings,

thankfully.

"I'll get it!"

I run to the living room and pick up the white receiver.

"Whatcha doing right now?" says Connie on the other end.

"Just finishing up pancakes. Why? What are you doing right now?"

"I just was thinking that maybe we could take our bikes down to Seven Springs. Think you could go?"

Bike riding OR Saturday morning chores that I know I have to do today?

The choice is clear.

"Mom, it's Connie! EVERYBODY is going to take off and have a picnic down at Seven Springs."

"Everybody?" Mom says with raised eyebrow. She knows me oh, so well.

"Well, sort of. We're just organizing everyone right now. Please? I'll do Saturday chores after I get back!"

She smiles.

"The bathroom needs to get scrubbed, and Dad wants you to wash the car when he gets home."

Of course. "Clean cars drive better," says The-Dad-Who-Knows-All.

"Think you will be back home before Dad finishes eighteen holes of golf?" says Mom with a grin.

I take that as a "YES" and make plans to meet up with "everyone" on the corner.

*This is one more reason to just love
Saturdays, especially when Saturday is
a Spontaneous Saturday. Chores have
to get done, sure, but you have to
play when you have to play,
especially when one RF Lichty is away.*

Connie did well organizing "everyone."

Francie and Greta are already peddling their bikes towards Connie's tiny house down the block. I hurry on my bike to catch up with them.

"Good thing you called! I got out of bathroom-scrubbing for a while," I say.

"How'd you get out of that so easily? Usually you're the only one who can't go anywhere unless chores are done," says Francie.

"It's because Dad's playing golf. If he were home, I would have a bucket and sponge in my hand right now." They laugh. They know my dad.

Peddling our bikes as if we owned the road, we take off to the magical place way at the end of Freeborn Street.

Seven Springs.

Following the blacktop past Skunk Hollow, up the dirt road, we look for the field beyond the fence, a field that contains large trees leaning over the ponds that spit up clear, white sand from the earth below. It's the place that gives so many of us kids a place to cool off, dream, and giggle, alone or with friends.

Carefully steering our bikes on the gravel road, we park them just outside a white gate that opens to a huge field. We make our way to the side of a pond. There, shoes come off, toes dip into the cool water, and we lie back. We feel the warm sun on our faces, and see clouds that look like huge mounds of whipped marshmallow against the Minnesota blue sky.

"What do you think about that movie yesterday?" starts Greta.

She giggles. Greta's giggle is a great giggle to have. "I heard that all the boys thought all of us girls had suddenly vanished."

"How'd you know that?" counters Connie.

"Because I talked to Bill Orcutt. He said that all the guys wondered why all the girls were gone."

Of course Greta would have talked to the boys.

"So they didn't even know what we were seeing?" I say.

Yesterday I could not have been more embarrassed seeing anyone of the opposite sex after watching *You're a Young Lady Now*. I just knew that they knew what I wish they didn't know.

"We should have told them it's all about Choonas," Connie laughs.

That's Connie's contribution to what we know about sex. Yes. Girl parts to her are "choonas." That term comes from . . . I don't know where . . . but you will never convince her to call "it" anything except a "choona."

"No! Better yet! When you talk to those guys, Greta, tell them in Pig Latin that we saw a film about "Oonachoos," I counter.

Greta laughs. We all convulse.

"Or how about "The Oonachoo Factory?"

We laugh until our sides hurt.

Life could not be better on this most perfect Saturday.

It's the Holstein cows that change the trajectory of the day, those cows that are just munching grass and doing the usual cow thing. Upon further observation, a couple of them are doing something I have not seen before. I squint and point it out to the others.

"What's up with those cows? It looks like one cow is trying to get up on the back of the other cow," I say.

"It's having a hard time doing it. Maybe it's a new kind of cow dance," Francie observes.

"Or maybe it's a new kind of cow back scratching move," Greta adds.

All alternatives are explored. When none seem plausible all eyes then go to me.

"Ask your Mom, Jane," orders Greta.

"Why me?" I reply.

"Because your mom tells you stuff," says Francie.

That part is true. She not only answers questions but also volunteers information even when I am not asking for any.

"Yep, like when she told you that you were going to have a little baby in the family."

I indeed did remember. That moment is seared in my memory even if I was only in about first grade.

I had been standing in Mom and Dad's bedroom when

Mom asked the question.

"Janie, would you like to have a baby brother or sister?"

(What if I had said, "No, actually I am content to be the baby of the family. I like my birth order."?)

Mom proceeded to tell me that there was a baby growing inside her tummy, right that very minute, and wasn't that wonderful?

Being inquisitive I had asked her, "How'd a baby get inside there?"

The subject of eggs was introduced at that point ("Not the kind we get at the egg farm") and how Daddy had to get the egg growing with some magical stuff.

"Dad has his man parts that put the magical stuff on the egg and there you go: BABY," was what I learned from this conversation.

It also raised another question in my mind that I had to ask Mom.

"How'd that stuff get past your girdle?"

I sure didn't remember her ever NOT wearing one of those. Mom assured me that she did not wear her girdle during those "Magic Moments."

That's why I'm asked to report on the Cow Dance.

We ride our bikes back up Freeborn Street, part ways, and I put my bike away in the garage underneath Alan's sign that he wrote on the garage wall. It said, "NO GRILS ALLOWED."

Dad is back from the golf game with Mr. Grangaard. I see the car parked on the side lawn waiting for me to get that chore done. Mom is in the living room doing her deskwork. She greets me and says that I can make a sandwich and then start on my chores. I try, unsuccessfully, to convince her to take me to Maid Rite instead. ("But Mom, you get five of those burgers for only a buck! Here. Just call Hemlock 3-6247. That could be dinner!")

I love those Maid Rites. I could eat all five myself.

She doesn't budge, even if it is a deal. Now I have to stop stalling and ask about the Cow Dance. I explain what we saw at Seven Springs.

Mom laughs.

"Cow Dance?" and then asks if I want to get my dad's take on this topic.

"He graduated in animal husbandry, honey, and was raised with farm animals. He knows a lot."

I think these kinds of topics are "Mom and Jane" time. ONLY Mom and Jane time. To involve Dad in these kinds of talks is making my insides as nervous as a fart on a hot skillet.

Mom persists. She can be like a homing pigeon when she is on a mission.

"Bob! Are you busy right now? Janie has a question for you, about Dancing Cows."

Dad turns around and looks at me with laughing eyes. He must have had a good golf game with Mr. Grangaard.

I can tell Mom and Dad are having great fun with this talk.

"Does it have anything to do with 'Five-legged horses'?" he says.

I cringe at that memory. I was much younger when I saw an excited horse alongside the highway as we were on our way to visit Grandpa Bechtelheimer. It just looked to me like the horse had another leg, even if it was a short one.

Dad then gets to the point when Mom explains the situation.

"That's how cows make calves," and then he starts going into detail.

The red flush starts to creep up my cheeks. I decide right then and there this is the last time I am coerced into those "Jane, Ask-Your-Mother" moments. The Freeborn Street chums will have to find out about Cow Dances on their own.

*But I did have to share with the girls
one tidbit I got from Dad years later.
He had said simply, "Put sex in a
bank, let it collect interest and
the dividends will pay off."*

Food.

Banking.

Golf.

If I can sum up "RFL" (that's how he signs things...it's short for Robert Fay Lichty), I can say that he is usually in "F" (food), "B" (banking), or "G" (golfing) mode. Sometimes he can be in all three modes simultaneously. That is not to say that he is in these modes ALL the time. However, from my vantage point, he is in these modes MOST of the time.

Food or "F" mode usually starts right at the breakfast table. After eating breakfast, he asks the same question: "What's for dinner tonight?"

How can you think of dinner when you just had breakfast?

Dad even uses the "F" mode to size up potential hires for the bank. He likes to invite them out for lunch, and observes how quickly they order from the menu. It's a good thing if the potential hire orders quickly. (He tells me that's a sign of being decisive.)

Banking, or "B" mode, is almost 24/7 with RFL. It's with him the minute his flat feet hit the floor in the morning until he puts them back into bed at night. "F" mode can feed the stresses of "B" mode. When he comes home around 4:00 or 5:00 at night, he will raid the refrigerator. If there is any Hormel Thuringer sausage in there, by 5:15, it could be gone. Mom knows that Dad will inhale that whole tasty sausage faster than a Hoover vacuum. He sabotages her efforts to control sausage attacks by volunteering to help with "quality taste control" at Hormel. He does a lot of "quality taste control." Mom can't seem to win at controlling Dad's girth expansion.

"You know what Mayo Clinic told you on your last physical, Robert."

"Ann. I know. I'm up seven pounds," Dad remarks as he cuts another hunk of sausage. "The good doctor also told me that it's evenly distributed."

I look at the cans of Metrecal that Mom bought for Dad last week.

"You could have this instead, Dad!" I say as I hold up the can of liquid meal replacement.

"That doesn't work, honey," says Mom. "That's one of the reasons he's up seven pounds. He drinks a meal in a can before a meal."

Dad glares. He knows Mom is right. She knows, too, that "B" mode can fuel "F" mode a lot.

That's why he needs a lot of golfing or "G" mode. Chasing that little white ball around eighteen holes makes him have to focus and concentrate on stance, drives, putts, and keeping his head down when he swings. A great "G" day usually happens when there is a less stressful "B" day. ("That's why golf is a head game, Jane," he says to me on occasion.) However, a bad "G" can fuel an attack of "F" when he is thinking about "B." "F" really goes into action when there is a stressful "G" day caused by worry about "B." Eating to live then becomes living to eat some days for one RFL.

"So what's for dinner?" says Dad.

"Torsk."

"Poor Man's Lobster, eh? What are we having with it?"

Mom is trying to get into healthy eating. She calls torsk "Poor Man's Lobster" to make it sound wonderful. She puts pieces of cod into boiling water that has some sugar thrown in to sweeten it up. (I throw more sugar into the water when she's not looking.) It's not bad if you drench each bite of boiled cod in a bowl of melted butter. Both Dad and I know that torsk can go from "healthy" to "artery clogging," depending on how much butter drenching we do.

"I have some rice that I'm mixing with the cooked spinach."

Mom is really proud of this side dish. She mixes white cooked rice with cooked spinach and presses it into a circular mold. She pops it into the oven until a crust forms on the top. Then she loosens the "Green Rice," puts it on a plate and puts steamed carrot rounds in the middle of it. The presentation is good and she gets us to eat both green and yellow veggies in one sitting.

Dad is in a rather good mood. He eyes the Thuringer with renewed vigor, and is about ready to slice another hunk of the sausage when we hear a knock at the back door.

"Jack! Come in!"

In walks one of our family's favorite friends. Jack and his

wife Mary go to our same church. Mom and Mary are charter—yes, CHARTER—members of the Christian Sisters' Bridge Club. Mary has told me that I may call her "Mary" instead of "Mrs. Strong."

I feel very honored.

The bond with the Strongs is deep, even though it got tested with last summer's vacation to Florida.

Mom and Mary had decided it would be fun to drive to Florida with all of us, kids included. Dad and Jack needed time away from work, and what better way to have family bonding time than taking a trip? We had never been that far away from Austin before, and the summer seemed a perfect time to make that dream happen. Piled into two cars, we had all left Austin for the Sunshine State. I'm not sure how Mary and Mom got everything organized, but they did. It was perfectly executed up until we got to Miami.

Tired from the long drive, we checked into the Carousel Motel. The carousel in the front was charming, but what was magical was having ocean just steps away from the back. All of us were anxious to experience the biggest body of water we had ever seen, jellyfish and all. Tall swaying palm trees, the roar of the mighty waves, the feel of the sun on my face—it could not have been a more perfect spot.

"We need an extra cot," Mom had announced to Dad as we were getting situated in our motel room. Dad stuck a cigar in his mouth and marched off to the motel office and asked for one.

"There will be a slight charge for the cot, Mr. Lichty," said the man behind the front desk.

"How much extra?"

"Five dollars for the cot, pillow, and sheets, sir."

"Five bucks? For that?" said Dad indignantly. There were no deals to be had concerning a cot. Not that my dad didn't try.

He came back to the room, and told Mom to pack up. We were going to have to find a cheaper place to stay. And that was that.

Jack, Mary, and their boys were not happy. Jack said something to Dad about, "Lichty, you are so tight you couldn't shoot a flax seed up your ass with a ten pound canon." All of us glared at Dad, who was not going to let up on finding another place to stay. We drove around and around the city, and finally, late at night, found a dumpy room at half the price. At that point, Mom was not talking to Dad. The kids were not talking to Dad. Jack and Mary were far from thrilled with him as well.

*Friends. They're treasures.
I think of the Girl Scout song I
learned with Mrs. Seiver and Mom
when they led our Brownie Scout
troop. It went: "Make new friends
but keep the old, One is silver and
the other gold." Indeed.*

The timing of a visit could not have been better. Dad forgets about Saturday chores, and is in good humor after Jack pops his head in the back door. After he leaves, though, it's back to business.

"Jane, set the table please," Mom asks of me.

"How come Alan can't help set the table? He's home now!"

"He's got a job to do. He has to rake up all those leaves."

I comply since Studley isn't around, and wonder when Betsy-the-Younger will start getting chores.

The table is set, and we all assume our positions at the Round Dining Room Table.

"Jane, pick a prayer," comes another Camp Bulletin.

I pull out the Blue Prayer Book and randomly choose the dinner prayer.

"Our Heavenly Father, in simple trust we say: This is the day that the Lord hath made, let us be glad in it. May we all be warm in heart and calm in spirit, trusting in the strength that comes from thee to keep us ever in the way of righteousness. In Jesus's name we pray. Amen."

I see Dad's eyebrows knit together.

Why?

Mom serves the torsk with individual bowls of butter. She knows we love to drench and savor each bite of the sweetened cod.

Dad finishes the torsk and generous helping of green

rice, puts his fork on the plate and grins.

"I heard a good one today about the new priest at St. Edward's Catholic Church."

We all lean forward.

"Father Andrew, the old priest, was handing over the reins to the young priest that was to take his place. And it was the first Sunday that the new priest was to deliver the homily.

"Naturally, this new priest was a bit nervous. He had some big shoes to fill and knew that Father Andrew would be listening and critiquing his performance."

Dad's eyes are twinkling.

"Father Andrew told the young priest not to be nervous. Just take a little swig out of the communion cup and he would be fine. The young priest did just that. And by the time he was ready to deliver the homily, that young priest was feeling mighty fine, mighty confident, and was looking out at a packed house.

"One by one, everyone starts to leave St. Edward's. The young priest looked out at an empty parish, empty except for one person sitting in the last pew."

Dad was gasping now, laughing even before he could get the words out. "Only one person was left in the sanctuary and that one person was Father Andrew."

"'What have I done?' asked the young priest. 'Why did everyone leave?'"

All of us are now trying to really understand Dad's

words because he's laughing so much.

The green rice is getting cold on my plate.

"'Oh, my son, my son. You made three tragic errors,' Father Andrew said."

"'First, David did not screw Goliath, he SLEW Goliath!'"

By now, we are almost on the floor.

"'Second,'" gasps Dad, tears flowing freely down his cheeks, "'Our Lord and Savior Jesus Christ was not circumcised on the cross for our sins; he was CRUCIFIED!'"

Our family can hardly wait for the last mistake. It's taking awhile for Dad to spit it out at this point. He finally does.

"And third, Fr. Andrew told the young priest, 'When you did the announcements, you told everyone that there was going to be a Peter Pull at St. Taffy's next Sunday after church!'"

Those stories, sprinkled with the humor, pulled us out of the pits more times than I can count. Maybe that's why Mom told me years later, "I fell in and out of love many times during my life, Janie. Thank God it was always with the same man."
Now I see why.

Winning by Default

"So what did you say was for dessert, Ann?"

"I didn't say, actually. What I was hoping for is that we burn the leaves in the driveway and make some s'mores."

I love the fall. When Dad rakes up a huge pile of maple leaves from the lawn to burn, it turns into a neighborhood gathering. Standing around the bonfire, talking and laughing, we have much discussion on the art of marshmallow browning.

I learn that the secret to a perfectly toasted marshmallow is to find those embers in the fire that you hold your stick close to. Then, all you need is patience. Out comes a perfectly bronzed, sugary mound that oozes together with the chocolate you put on top. Then, when you press two graham crackers over the gooey sweetness and eat it by the heat of the bonfire, life is about as good as it can get.

"I bet we can rake a pile together faster than you can get the dishes done!" challenges Dad.

I don't mind clearing the table and think Mom and I can easily finish our chore before the guys get the leaves piled.

However, I get sidetracked.

"Mom, what's this?" I ask as I pull out a card I find lying on the windowsill.

I know. I should have been clearing the table.

"It's just a card from Johnny Mayer that I kept. He gave us that for our anniversary."

I am really intrigued. He wrote a poem about Mom and Dad inside the card.

I start to read:

> *We have always thought that Bob and Ann Lichty*
> *were not only a lovely couple, but are perfectly*
> *compatible. For example:*
>
> *When Bob is impulsive, Ann is patient*
> *When Ann is impulsive, Bob is delighted.*
>
> *When Bob drinks too much, Ann gets tired.*
> *When Ann drinks too much, Bob is surprised.*
>
> *When Bob is hungry, Ann is on a diet.*
> *When Ann is hungry, Bob is too!*
>
> *When Bob is golfing, Ann is sympathetic.*
> *When Ann is sympathetic, Bob is disgusted.*
>
> *When Ann is romantic, Bob is tired.*
> *When Bob is romantic, Ann is surprised!*

"Jane! You shouldn't read our card!" She goes to snatch the card from my hand.

I run.

Mom starts to run after me. "You cannot outrun your

mother, Jane Ann!"

"Bet I can!" I laugh and go outside with the card in my hand.

"What's going on?" Dad asks with the rake in his hand.

I reply. "Mom doesn't think that I can outrun her, Dad."

That's all it took for my dad to put down the rake.

He's grinning at Mom.

She is not grinning back.

"So you think I can't run any more Bob Lichty?" retorts Mom with her hands on her hips.

"I didn't say that!"

"Well, I can run as fast as Jane."

Actually, Mom can.

Dad rubs his chin and starts to grin.

"OK. How about a little challenge, girls?"

I am stupefied. I have never seen Mom with this competitive edge.

Smiling at her I ask, "Are you sure you want to do this Mom?"

"Yes, I do! And please give me back our card!"

Dishes left on the table, card put away, Mom and I get a Camp Bulletin on how the race is to proceed.

Both Mom and I are to stand at the northeast corner of the house. When Dad says, "Go!" Mom is to run clockwise around the house twice, and I am to run counterclockwise as many times.

First one to get back to the corner wins.

Simple. Mom and I get ready.

"Runners, on your mark, get set, GO," Dad bellows.

I pass Mom at the southwest corner of the house. I look at her and she is laughing. Me too.

I go around a second time.

No Mom is to be seen.

I sprint to the finish line.

"Where's Mom?" I ask Dad.

He is laughing so hard I have trouble understanding him.

"She had to quit."

"Why?"

"Because..." Dad wipes away the tears from his eyes with a gloved hand, "your mother wet her pants during the second lap. She was laughing too hard."

That's a lesson in and of itself.

Never race without emptying your bladder first.

The pile of leaves is ready to be torched, and I am ready to make s'mores. I am over the patient method of making them and go for efficiency. Set that sucker on fire, let it burn and blow it out. Charred is not bad with chocolate, anyway, especially eating it while looking at a great sunset framing the last moments of a good day on Freeborn Street.

It's those small moments that count.
Just like charred marshmallows,
some moments can look so ugly on the
outside. But you miss out on a
wondrous bite of life if you don't
savor the goodness that's on the inside.

SUNDAY

1957

Three Squeezes

Nope, not that one either.

I throw yet another outfit on the floor. I have to find a "Sunday" something to wear to church. I can't wear play clothes or a regular everyday dress or skirt. No, it has to be a "Going to Church" outfit.

Maybe I'll wear one of the jumpers Mom made.

She makes many of the clothes I have, to save money. Jumpers are her forte. I have a jumper in most of the basic colors. Put on a white blouse and I'm good to go.

Mom has this "Going to Church" drill down pat: girdle, bra, nylons, and slip?

Check.

Good grey suit, pearl earrings, and heels?

Check.

Pot roast, peeled potatoes, carrots, and onions in the Dutch oven?

Check.

Kids with hair combed, clean teeth, shined shoes?

Almost check.

Dad in the car blowing on the horn five minutes before we're supposed to leave?

Check.

Lutherans, Catholics, and Protestants alike, the drill is almost the same at every home in Austin. Every Sunday you just go to church.

I remember asking Mom why we didn't go to the same

church as Connie and Greta.

"Everyone plows different furrows but we're all trying to get to the same side of the field. That's what Grampa Lichty used to say. And we like going to this church."

No matter what furrow people plow, Sunday going to church is usually at the same time. There is never a day of rest in our house.

I put on the saddle shoes that Dad shined on Saturday. That's his job. Heaven forbid we should wear scuffed up shoes to church. My siblings are already downstairs, halos in place because they have already eaten some cereal and are ready to go out to the car.

"I'm coming!" I yell, flying out the door with a piece of toast in my hand. I know that after church the fellowship hall has coffee and goodies, so I know I won't starve.

Maybe Betty Barber will make those toffee bars for coffee hour.

A blast on the car horn announces Dad's impatience for us to get going.

"Get in! We're late!" his voice booms as we get in the car. He's not as happy as he was last night. I take this personally.

It's quiet in the car with Dad at the wheel, grinding his teeth.

Most Sundays I love the drive to the First Congregational Church. It's new. I love the sprawling red brick building with its white steeple. I love all the lush, green grass that is always perfectly mowed. Most...I love the people that go there. I know most everyone, and like it or not, most everyone knows me.

This Sunday it's a little strained in the car going to church.

I wasn't five minutes early getting in the car. I bet that's why he's grinding his teeth.

Dad drives in the church parking lot, and lets Mom out at the front door. She makes a beeline to the choir room to practice the offertory song and get into her choir robe before the service.

I edge myself towards the sanctuary.

"There's the Strongs and the Spahns, Dad. Near the front. Can't we sit by them?"

"Nope," says Alan. You know where we always sit."

I know. It's always in the back row.

"Why can't we sit in the front? Then I could see Mrs. Dewey's feet play on the organ pedals!"

I love the way she uses her feet on the organ pedals. She's amazing. Her fingers fly over two rows of keyboards, occasionally pulling out some knobs, while both feet are going all over the place, her body leaning back and forth. It is a total body effort to get every song to sound so beautiful.

"Because Dad can see who would really like to be a new customer of the bank, that's why," answers Alan.

No wonder assets of First National Bank are on the rise. In-

stead of listening to sermons he's busy cultivating accounts.

I know then we will be sitting right behind Jim and Laura Huntting. They always sit in the pew right in front of us.

I'm right.

Mr. Huntting graciously lets Mrs. Huntting in first. I position myself behind Mrs. Huntting. She's a whole lot shorter than Mr. Huntting.

Maybe Mrs. Huntting made her famous brownies for coffee today. Those would go well with Betty Barber's toffee bars.

My stomach is growling a little.

"Morning Bob, Kids," says Mr. Huntting. "You passing the plate today, Bob?"

"Nope, not today," says Dad.

"Too bad," Mr. Huntting smiles. "We always get more money in it when you pass it."

Dad grins.

"How's that?" I ask.

"Your dad was on the building fund back when we had to raise money for a new church. He'd take the offering up, like a good usher does, and look in the plate. If the plate didn't have enough money in it, he'd turn around and pass the plate again."

I roll my eyes.

Mrs. Huntting turns around to address us.

"Robert, stop by with the family this afternoon. I just made some brownies."

Yes! Toffee bars first . . . then . . . the brownies . . . after the bars have a chance to settle. Life is good!

Dad's ready to say something back but is stopped by the first chords coming from the organ. Mrs. Dewey is working her musical magic, and once again does not disappoint. The choir lines up two by two behind us and starts the processional to the front of the church.

The alto section seems really strong today. That's Mom's section.

However, the quantity of altos still is not enough to overpower Mrs. Huntting's distinctive voice. She likes to sing with a lot of gusto.

The choir makes it to the choir loft just as the last notes of the anthem leave the organ.

It's pretty much the same every Sunday. A processional, a few anthems, sermon by the current reverend, pass the plate, finish with the choir going back to where they started, and the church part is pretty much done. I sit with the family, draw, look at what kids are in church, and observe Dad resting his elbow on the end of the pew. He doesn't seem to be into sermons very much.

I wish Mom still sat with us instead of with the choir.

I miss the Secret Squeeze. When I would get the squirmies during sermons Mom would place her hand in mine and squeeze it three times. It's her secret way of saying "I love you."

Then I would squeeze her hand twice. That means,

"How much?"

She then would squeeze my hand really hard. I would sometimes wince at all the "loveness." But it told me I was really loved.

No more squeezes now that she's in the choir.

I should be listening to Rev. Arnold's sermon but visions of Betty Barber's toffee bars keep racing in my mind. The stomach growlies are getting louder.

I look at the back of the heads of the Spahn family.

Isn't it weird that Mr. Spahn and Dad even went to Iowa State together and here they both end up in Austin?

I think of the story Dad told me of driving to the Spahns when Mrs. Spahn was ready to deliver. Dad almost drove his car through their front door in his haste to drive Mrs. Spahn to the hospital in time. They named the baby "Bobbie" instead of "Mary" to honor my Dad.

Good thing Mrs. Dewey is starting to play the recessional. Hope she plays full throttle.

She does.

"How Great Thou Art" has a lot of stanzas in it, especially when you want to be the first one in the fellowship hall for "Meet, Greet, and Eat" time. To my chagrin, it's taking the choir a long time to get back down the aisle.

Finally they stand around the back of the church to sing the benediction:

The Lord bless you and keep you

The Lord lift his countenance upon you.
And give you peace.
And give you peace.
Ah ah ah Men
Ah ah ah Men
Ah ah ah Men

They're really into a lot of Ah-ah-ah-mens...hope they wrap it up soon.

Dad's really antsy. He's penned in by the choir so his quick exit to get to the fellowship hall first is thwarted. When we do get there, I notice the white tablecloths are pressed to perfection, and trays of delectable goodies are perfectly positioned so parishioners can take one to have with coffee or juice. Some take just one. If Betty Barber's toffee bars are there I plan on taking more than just one.

Yes. You can call me "Piggy."

I search each platter.

What? No bars?

I am beyond dismayed.

My stomach says take what you can get so I reach for a couple of oatmeal raisin cookies. Those are not my favorite but they will have to suffice.

"Hungry?" says my brother. He knows perfectly well I am.

Mrs. Huntting stands by us with her coffee in hand. I think of the brownies in my future.

"Alan Lichty! You're taller than your dad!"

Alan beams.

"Almost" he says.

"Well, you have come a long way since you handed the car keys to your dad in church long ago."

My ears perk up.

Mrs. Huntting can talk. A lot. When she tells a story there is a great quantity of detail. Be prepared to listen awhile.

I am prepared.

"What's that story, Mrs. Huntting?"

"It was when you were a baby, Jane, and your family was still living in the rental on Winona Street. Yes, the very house where your brother liked to dig under the fence, ditch his clothes and run naked across the street. Your poor mother was frantic most of the time.

"Well," Mrs. Huntting has to take a deep breath to continue, "Your dad had gone to church. It was in the old Congregational Church downtown then, while your mom stayed at home with you."

My brother is looking a little uncomfortable right now, but is too polite to leave. He shifts from one leg to another. I love it.

"Well, you, Alan, made an unexpected entry during Rev. Vance's very somber sermon. As I recall most of the congregation was in attendance that Sunday, and Alan, you could not have picked a better moment to announce to everyone's surprise—as well as to the embarrassment of some, 'Dad! Dad! Here are your car keys! Let's go home!'"

"No bullet ever left the barrel of a gun faster than did one Robert Lichty as he left his seat in the sanctuary and escorted you outside, Alan."

Alan turns red. By now many are crowded around the cookies to hear Mrs. Huntting's story of the car keys.

"And, if I remember right, George Vance's sermon needed a little lift," says Dad as he reaches for another cookie.

Dad actually listened to a sermon?

I'm amazed. There might be more going on in his head than growing a bank's assets.

*It wasn't just Betty Barber's bars
or Laura Huntting's stories that kept
me going Sunday after Sunday.
More, it was that community of faith
residing in that church,which gave not
just Dad but our whole family a
foundation on which to stand.
It's a foundation that has helped me
weather almost everything that has
come my way.*

Pot Roast and Persistance

"Smells good Mom," I say, inhaling the aroma that fills the house. It's Mom's never-fail pot roast. Carrots, potatoes, and onions are added to the roast she buys at Richard's Meat Market. Seasoned to perfection and slow-cooked in Mom's magical cast iron Dutch oven, the marriage of flavors is a favorite Sunday dinner.

Ann Lichty, "Annie-Bun Buns," is a superb cook, I have to say. Maybe everything tastes so good because of the "Love" ingredient she adds to each and every dish. Or maybe it's just how she approaches cooking as an art.

"Some ingredients," she told me once, "can be savored as is . . . like a tomato pulled fresh from the vine. But sometimes that tomato needs a little something to make it taste better, like a little bit of sugar or salt."

Mom could be the tomato, good as is. Big Bob on the other hand, needs some seasoning help.

She continued. "When you put good ingredients together, give them a chance to blend their flavors. I find that it never fails to make something wonderful."

"Just like people," she adds with a smile.

I'm thinking that some people don't blend so well . . . like brothers. Little sisters are OK.

"Wash up!" roars Dad. "Let's eat!"

Hands are washed and once again we sit at that Round Dining Room Table with the indestructible top. It's a little quiet at first as we all dig in, knowing that Mom is not going to be cooking at all after today's meal. On Sundays we are on our own after Sunday dinner.

Maybe that's why we like to go out and visit friends on Sundays. We're always offered something to eat.

"So, would you go for the 'A' or settle for the 'C,' Jane," Dad finally breaks the silence as he pours a little au jus over his potatoes.

"Huh?" I reply. I have no idea what my father is talking about.

"The sermon. Weren't you listening?"

I confess. I wasn't.

"Too bad. It was one of Ed Arnold's finer sermons."

"I thought it was too," says Mom.

Now I wish I had paid more attention to the sermon than to the pink slippers Mrs. Dewey was wearing when she played the organ. I am amazed at how adept I am at tuning things out. Not a skill I should have been practicing during Ed Arnold's sermon, apparently.

"Could you refresh my memory what he talked about?" I ask nicely.

Alan smirks.

Mom fills me in.

"Well, Rev. Arnold talked about a final test that a class had to take. I think he said it was in an English class."

I reach for another piece of roast. I'm not quite onboard with the significance of Ed Arnold's sermon.

Mom continues. "Well, they have these Blue Books that

students write in to answer essay questions when they take their final." I'm not connecting to this at all. No wonder I wasn't listening.

"So, this college teacher, let's call him Dr. Clayson, passes them out and tells the kids not to open up those Blue Books, but just put their names on the front of them."

I take the perfect bite of roast, carrot, and potato all on the fork. Those flavors just go together so well.

"This college professor did something that had not been done before. He passed out the Blue Books to the class and told them that they really didn't have to take the final."

I like this professor.

"That is, if you wanted a sure 'C' in the class."

I know what having a "C" means. It means just about average. It means you can do better, says my Dad. He said one time he was happy getting a "C" in organic chemistry when he went to Iowa State. He was sweating that grade a lot. Maybe it was because he spent too much time waiting tables in a girls' sorority.

"So, half the class passed their Blue Books back in and walked out, happy to have the 'C' instead of risking flunking the final. They were happy," says Mom.

"They took the easy way out," interjects Dad, sopping up the rest of the au jus with a roll.

There is a lesson here. I can just feel it.

"Well, the ones that stayed behind in the class were told

to open up their Blue Books to the last page. On that page was written a huge 'A."

"Why?" I ask.

"You would know if you had listened!" says dear Alan.

"Alan. Stop," says Mom. "Let me finish."

"Their professor told the rest of the class they got an 'A,'" she continues, "because they stayed."

There's that lesson.

Mom smiles. She knows me. Yes, I would have taken the sure thing. I know that about me.

I get it.

I think it goes back to the thing about over-prepare and then go with the flow. I know that if I can't let my brilliance dazzle, I will sometimes fall back on "Bullshit bafflement." (That's what Dad calls it.) Sometimes, though, I don't want to over-prepare. That's where I am not at all like my dad.

"I don't know what the big deal is about grades. Look at Thomas Edison. He was at the bottom of his class and he did just fine in life," I spear the last bite of carrot on my plate.

"Jane has a point, Bob. Even one of the Mayo brothers was not so good at reading and spelling. They've done well at the clinic."

Of course they have. Those boys had to learn another language by the time they were my age, had to read a book a week and couldn't watch more than an hour of TV a week.

94

"You aren't getting what Arnold was saying," says Dad. "Those guys did well because they persisted, and didn't give up. That's what I mean by going for the 'A.'"

Dad scores on that one. He is like a bulldog when he goes after something. "You have to have tenacity," he says. "And I'll take that over someone who just does the job half way."

Dad pushes back his chair, and issues the "Clear off the table" Camp Bulletin. He goes in to finish reading the Sunday edition of the the *Austin Daily Herald* and the *Minneapolis Star Tribune*.

I'd like to just look at the funnies to see the *Peanuts* strip.

And then, "Ann, I talked with Laura Huntting and she talked about us going over this afternoon to visit."

"She did? Well, I talked to Janet Plager. She invited us over to have popcorn while we watch the *Ed Sullivan Show.*"

"Figure it out and let me know," he says as he clamps his teeth down on a cigar. How he can stand those things is beyond me. How Mom can stand those things is beyond me.

I think of Mom and the jobs she does: cook, meal planner, arbitrator, scheduler, bill payer, hostess, all in addition to being wife and mother.

Yep. Mom would be the 'A' person
Ok...Dad would be too.

I think of that lesson a lot when I would
like to do just a half-hearted job.
I remember what a coach of
Notre Dame, Lou Holtz, said one time.
He told his football team that he had
three rules for them, and they'd best
follow them. They were off the team if
they didn't.
Those rules were:
1. Do your best. Some days your best is
not as good as other days
but still give it all you can.
2. Do right.
3. Treat the other guy
the way you want to be treated.

I think Big Bob and Lou Holtz would
have gotten along really well.

"Get ready to go, kids," barks Dad.

Yes. Even on Sundays. Camp Bulletins still persist.

"Did you call Hunttings and tell them I'll stop by and see them during the week?" Dad asks.

"I did, and Plagers said come over when we're ready."

This makes Sunday night a good night, even without Mrs. Huntting's brownies.

It's become a ritual of sorts going over to the Plagers' to watch the *Ed Sullivan Show* on their small black and white TV. It's the popcorn, however, that makes that viewing so memorable. Mrs. Plager makes the best popcorn I have yet to eat. She makes it on their stove, in what I call the magic popcorn pan. She puts Crisco, or something like it, in the pan and when it melts, she puts just a few kernels in that hot oil. Not too many and not too few. When she hears the first "POP," she adds more and then starts moving that pan back and forth, focused, not missing a moment of movement until all the popping is done.

The smell is heavenly. Topped with melted butter, that popcorn becomes borderline divine.

Actually, anything topped with melted butter is borderline divine.

The Plagers have been friends forever, it seems. Mrs. Plager makes this wonderful Christmas Braid that she delivers every Christmas like clockwork. I look forward to Christmas morning when we can devour it after opening our presents. I learned what made the Plager family so special at one of those devourings.

"I had a job in Humboldt, Iowa, as a county agricultural agent after I graduated from Iowa State College," Dad said. "Carroll—Mr. Plager—knew that the bank in Austin needed an 'ag guy' in the loan department. He knew my name from a mutual friend and so he suggested me."

"What's an ag guy?" I knew nothing about ag guys.

"It's short for 'agriculture,' Jane," Mom filled in, like she had to do with me a lot. "Your dad grew up in farming, thought he would be a farmer, and so went to college to major in Animal Husbandry."

Wonder why they didn't call it Animal Wifery?

Dad then followed with a discourse about how one person that knew him in college at Ames knew another person and they all agreed Dad was a hard working guy that might do well in helping famers with loans.

"Did you know anything at all about banking?" I asked.

"That's why your dad went back to school, honey," interjected Mom.

Then I got it. I remembered when Dad had to go to Banking School in Madison, Wisconsin. It was after that Mom gave me the news that I was going to have a new sibling in the family. Yep. Nine months later after Banking School, Betsy-the-Younger came on the scene.

In short, Plagers were the ones that helped get Bob

Lichty on a banking trajectory, and the friendship grew from there.

The doorbell is rung at Plagers and we are ushered into their living room. The popcorn smell permeates every inch of their house so I know Mrs. Plager has been working on her popcorn magic.

"It's almost 7:00. Time for Ed," says Mr. Plager as he walks over to turn on the TV.

Howard Duff and Ida Lupino, George Burns and Gracie Allen, maybe Topo Gigio will all be on the program tonight. I'm happy to see that little puppet and am anxious to hear him say, "Keesame goo night" to Mr. Sullivan.

Mrs. Plager comes out with bowls of popcorn for everyone. I am hoping she put a little more butter on my bowl.

She did. She knows.

The parents and Plagers are not paying attention to the Ed Sullivan Show, however. They have some catching up to do in the adjoining room. I am wishing that they would talk more quietly so I could hear what Ida Lupino has to say about her husband, Howard Duff. I wonder if she'll answer the question why she's not Ida Duff instead of Lupino. Mom took Dad's last name. Thank goodness. If I were "Jane Ann Bechtelheimer" I would need a lot of room to write my name.

It's difficult to hear anything. The parents and the Plagers are not talking softly at all.

"How's the forum coming along, Bob?" asks Mrs. Plager.

Forum? What forum?

"Good. I'm glad you gave us the idea to have discussions on financial topics for women. We're lining up speakers now."

"When the bridge club got together we talked about some possible topics," says Mom.

I see Dad take another sip of the scotch that Mr. Plager gave him.

"Like?"

"Some said 'budgeting.' Some of the widows said they would like to know more about 'estate planning' and 'investing.'"

I have no idea what those things are. Get me back to George and Gracie!

George Burns is always the serious guy and Gracie delivers the comedy. I think they are a great team, right up there with Lucille Ball and Desi Arnaz.

I turn up the volume on the Plagers' black and white TV set, just in time to hear Gracie tell George about Thanksgiving.

"Well, you see George, one Christmas my father caught a wild turkey and he fed him corn and chestnuts."

"Corn and chestnuts, Gracie?"

"Yes George. And then we didn't have the heart to kill him. So we let him get away. But the turkey liked the food so well that he came back each year. And that way we always had..."

"A turkey for Christmas dinner?" asks George.

I laugh out loud.

The Plagers and the parents are missing the best line of all when Gracie says, "This used to be a government of checks and balances, George. Now it's just all checks and no balances."

Money stuff even on TV!

I think of Mom. I see her doing the bills. Maybe she should be in government because she balances the checkbook all the time. She does a good job making sure we get what we need with the money we have. Thanks goodness for those green stamps I have to lick and put in stamp books. We can trade them in for stuff that Mom thinks we need. Those stamps and the Singer sewing machine she uses to make school jumpers for me help make ends meet.

Money management must be on Dad's mind a lot these days. Maybe he didn't know when he got into banking how money counseling would be a huge part of his job. I think growing up in the Depression and getting evicted from a rental because his Dad didn't have money to pay the rent is what made Dad so frugal and careful.

Maybe that's why he says a hungry dog hunts better.

"I need to work on our daughter however," Dad says in a voice loud enough for me to hear.

Who? Me?

I think I don't want to overhear this part and should instead concentrate on what Ida Lupino has to say about her husband Howard Duff.

"I talked to her about having her own checking account last week. I'm a little worried about her money management skills. When Jane thinks of trips to Rochester, visions of buying clothes at Dayton's dance in her head," Dad shares with the Plagers.

He doesn't have to tell them that!

"If I can teach Jane about budgeting, I can teach anyone," continues Dad, laughing as he downs another gulp of scotch.

"I'll help her Bob," says Mom gently.

That's a good thing.

I know Dad is trying to teach me about how to budget. I remember when he sat me down last week and handed me a check addressed to me. Just me. He told me that out of that amount I would need money to save, some money to give, and the rest to spend on necessities. If there is money left over I could spend it on things I want, not necessarily need.

"What if I need to get a new coat or shoes?" I ask, knowing they cost more.

"You'll have to figure it out. How much do you think you'll need for clothes each month? How much do you need for school lunches? Movies? Going to the roller rink? Those are things you will have to make sure you have enough money for, as well as have money to save."

Huh?

"And if you haven't saved up for them, then figure out a way to earn money to buy it."

I should have listened. I should have asked.

Years later, bemoaning the lack of money for kids, mortgages and food, I called Dad. I told him that I was in trouble with credit cards because we were short of cash.

Me. A bankers' daughter. Not good, but I had to swallow a bunch of pride to seek help. I knew he helped many customers with the same dilemma.

"I told you years ago what this easy credit was going to do to people, Jane. It would get them in trouble," he replied.

That conversation at the Round Dining Room Table happened about the same time that a friend stopped being a friend because of Dad not giving the family a loan. He did that because he knew the family would have a tough time of trying to repay it and he didn't want them to lose a home because of it.

He also sent me a handwritten note, a note that I still have framed in my office.

It says:

> Dear Jane,
>   Enclosed is an interesting article. Under present tax laws there is no way any individual can make any money borrowing. It is real costly. You ask, How can

we ever buy anything?

It takes a real disciplined savings program over and above your retirement savings. By so doing you can pay cash when something unusual comes up. One really has to ask where the priorities mostly are.

Love,

Dad

There is a direct correlation between
happiness and a positive cash flow.
It took many years for me to know the
difference between "Wants" and "Needs."
It's been an essential lesson.

EPILOGUE
2014

Ripples

Lured by the smell and sight of rain, I open the door to the covered front deck of our home. I inhale the moisture in the air, welcoming it as I sit down in the wicker rocker. Dark clouds are gathering in the distance, pushing their way over and through the San Juan Mountain range that looms in front of me.

"We don't sit out here enough, Jane," Dick had said to me.

He's right. My mate of many years of marital ups-and-downs and in-betweens, and I have gotten to the point where we agree more than not.

Remember what Mom said in that last phone call?

I had told her that I was ready to trade Dick in for a new Hoover. Adjusting to retirement years was a bit of a challenge. She listened.

"I know you fell in and out of love with Dad. Well, I'm obviously in the 'Out' phase right now!" I complained.

"Well, just remember," Mom replied, "no matter the differences, if both of you were the same, Jane, one of you would be unnecessary!"

She knew just how to put me back on track.

How I miss her.

My mate interrupts the moment when he sits down in the matching wicker rocker.

"I have something for you."

And there it is.

An off-white rectangular envelope addressed to me. Just

me. It had come about a month after I first Googled this man named Garwin McNeilus, the name that was on the mudflaps. On impulse I had written him a note asking if he knew one "Bob Lichty."

He replied to me with a two-page, typed letter.

Wow.

I read it once. I have to read it again. There are too many tears that I have to wipe away as I try to absorb the words that are on them. They are words that, like the soft rain outside, help to wash away resentments of Camp Bulletins that have stuck in my craw for way, way too many years.

Dear Ms. Pearson,

Both Marilee and I will always be grateful to your dad for the role he played in our lives.

Very early in my career, I needed a loan in order to buy some used concrete mixer trucks for our small business. We were incredibly poor in those days and the survival of our business depended on securing this loan. I first went to our local bank in our hometown to apply for a loan and was turned down. I went to another nearby bank and we met with the same result. The situation was precarious for our small business.

He continued.

> I then went to the First National
> Bank of Austin where I was introduced
> to Bob Lichty. Bob was the president of
> that bank and he listened patiently as
> I explained our business plan and loan
> needs. How well I remember him looking
> over the top of his glasses at me and
> saying, 'Young man, you do not qualify
> for a loan on paper.'

I stop reading his letter for a moment.

*I do vaguely remember Dad telling us about this guy. Wonder
what made Dad and the loan department take a chance on him?*

> For some reason, said your father, "I
> believe in you, and will give you this
> loan provided you get a good lawyer to
> guide you legally." That lawyer I was
> told would be an attorney who repre-
> sented and advised me so well all these
> years since. Your dad also told me that
> I would need a good CPA and recommended
> one. Our family has used his services
> and those of his company ever since.

It was a good thing Dad gambled on him. Garwin was

feeding his family at that time using credit cards.

I continue reading and find that the gamble paid off. That banking relationship spanned many years. I learn that Garwin grew a tiny company into the McNeilus Truck and Manufacturing brand concrete mixers. He eventually held the vast majority of the mixer market across the entire United States, Mexico, and down through Central America.

But what he said next in his letter is something I shall never forget.

> We are not always able to see the full impact of our decisions and actions over the course of our lives. But in this case, it is possible to catch a small glimpse of the incredible good that came from your dad's belief in me and our small business venture.
>
> Although we sold McNeilus Truck and Manufacturing in 1998, the success realized as a result of that belief in me and our company has allowed us to help build over 15,000 churches, schools and orphanages around the world.

I remember long ago when Mom and I sat at the edge of East Side Lake in Austin throwing stones into the water. We watched the ripples spread out, wondering how far and how wide each thrown pebble and rock would go.

I think of those ripples now, the impact felt near and far by so many.

I think of the word legacy. I know now that each and every one of us has a capability of leaving one. It doesn't matter where we come from, but where we choose to go. It doesn't matter what we have, but what we choose to build.

I look at my husband and take his hand. The clouds have dissipated and those mountains once again are cloaked in blue skies.

Letting go of grudginess is a good thing. It's a very good thing.

I had assumed so many things about a very strict father that raised me during the '50s. Old fears, memories, and prejudices that filtered my perceptions of the man I called "Dad" (well, other things too!) began to change. Even Camp Bulletins began to take on a different hue other than "RED."

Growing up in the '50s was an interesting era to me. I grew up during a time when appearance was everything, and there were roles that each man and woman had to assume. But those seemingly smooth waters had an undercurrent, an undercurrent of much discontent. That discontent erupted during the '60s, and many, especially we women, had to wrestle with our roles in society. The rigid ropes of "acceptable" were starting to be loosened, and those uncharted waters were not easy ones to navigate. The lessons learned from that Round Dining Room Table at 1110 became a valuable rudder to me. They helped me navigate. No matter the storms, I would go back to the foundation that family provided.

The lessons of loyalty to family and friends, of seeking out the rewarding and enriching moments that each and every day can bring, of dealing fairly with all, learning how to entertain ourselves with not a whole lot except our imaginations, of not just wishing for something but planning and working for it—they all came from that street. "If wishes were horses beggars might ride" still echoes in my mind when I want to take the easy way out.

The lessons of building connections beginning in our homes, our neighborhoods, and our communities were right there in front of me at 1110 Freeborn Street. I didn't learn the Facebook kind of connection. I learned face-to-face, time spent getting the real kind of connection.

Years ago, I had stolen (yes, I did) Mom's address book and written to the many friends and family she had listed in that book. I asked for each to contribute a memory they had about my folks. The response I got was overwhelming. I compiled them into two huge albums and gave them to Mom and Dad for their 40th wedding anniversary.

Each of the letters that family and friends wrote gave me a different glimpse of the two people that helped grow me up. How treasured those letters were to them both, bringing back memories from early childhood in Orange Township to their involvement in the community of Austin. How treasured those letters are to our family now. Those letters became invaluable to me as I wrote this book.

PS. Guess what I just saw driving to PJ's Market? Yep . . . those mudflaps.

ACKNOWLEDGMENTS

"Keep going. Don't give up."

Those words came from many. I thank all of you. My childhood chums, Connie, Francie, and Greta, you have been a great resource of filling in where my memory has failed. Dr. Cheryl Clay, how lucky I am to have gotten to know you when we went to the Pike's Peak Writing Conference. The time on the Pine (River) and many meetings as writers have been a source of great joy. Becca Steinbach, "The Tea in the Woods" (with prosecco!) that you organized held many magical moments for me. I felt like Story Teller Extraordinaire sharing some words from 1110.

The need for a good editor is beyond measure. (Aunt Katherine's obit is a good case in point. It read: "As per her request there will be no *pubic* viewing." I should hope not.) Beth Green, you are a treasure. I have learned much about internal discourse versus reflection, correct verb tenses to go with each, and the countless rewrites that stretched and made me grow as a writer. (As an English minor at Macalester College years ago I missed some of those nuances.) You and Lisa Snider are a remarkable team, and I thank you for taking on my project.

Kathleen Shadell, what a talented wondrous soul you are, and to have your painting of 1110 is a treasure beyond compare. Thank you my friend.

The pen and ink drawing at the front of this book was given to me by a former student, Joanna Capelin. I never tire of looking at it, and have named this publishing venture in response to its message: keep dreaming, no matter the age, and let your dreams take flight.

Dick, how many times did you have to listen to another revision? It's been more *Fun with Dick and Jane* than not, and I'm so glad we chose each other to go through this life adventure together. Since you fished me out of Sig Creek, I'll renew our contract for many more years together! (Ok. Fine. I was going to do that anyway.)

To #1 Son Geoff and #1 Daughter Jennie and the Grandest of Grands, Abbie, Will, and Gabriella, thank you for being in my world. Each of you has a uniqueness that is a blessing to me. What would a life be without family? I know for me, my life has been enriched beyond measure by all of you.

REFERENCES

Clough, William A. *Father We Thank Thee: Graces for the House.* Abingdon Press. MCMXLIX

Snavely, Ida B. *Orange Township Lore.* 1958

Pearson, Jane. *A Book of Investments: A Collection of Letters for Big Bob and Annie Bun-Buns.* Privately published, 1980.

ABOUT THE AUTHOR

Jane Lichty Pearson, grandmother, mother and dreamer of honey-dos, is a re-purposed kindergarten teacher. She never sees a can of Spam without thinking about her childhood in Austin, Minnesota.